ROCHELLE HICKS

BrandCraft

Navigating the Heartbeat of Business Success

Contents

Preface

Hey fabulous folks, it's Rochelle here – your average small-shop enthusiast, seeker of hidden gems, and the queen of making friends everywhere I go. Now, before you raise those eyebrows and ask, "Why on earth is Ariel writing a book about Branding?" – let me spill the tea.

I might not be the CEO of multiple companies but, hear me out. My life revolves around those heartwarming connections, and when I shop, I'm not just swiping my card; I'm on a quest for those warm, fuzzy feelings. You know what I mean?

Think about it. Every Wednesday, I waltz into my favorite coffee joint, and it's not just about the lavender latte. No, no! I want to know who's conjuring up that magic – not just their job title and name but the real deal. And let me tell you, when I stroll into the pet boutique (my dog's paradise – bones everywhere!), the owner doesn't just greet my dog; they know my name too! Now, for fellow pet owners, you know that's a big deal – most people only remember the pet's name.

Why am I telling you all this? Because, my dear friends, people crave connections. Whether it's the Barista who crafts your caffeine masterpiece or the pet boutique owner who treats you and your furball like VIPs – it's about people connecting with people.

And that, my friends, is exactly what this book is about. So,
buckle up for a ride full of inspiration, a dash of humor, and a
guide to creating those unforgettable connections through your
brand. Because, let's face it, the world could use a little more
lavender lattes and dog-friendly boutiques in our lives. Cheers
to the joy of connecting!

1

Introduction

Branding isn't just about slapping logos on stuff; it's like stepping into a whole experience. Picture the brands you love – they're not just selling you a product or a service; they're pulling you into a world where every interaction sparks a feeling. It's like magic, but for businesses.

These legendary brands haven't just been selling stuff; they've been serving up an experience that's as reliable as your grandma's pie recipe, over years and decades. And you know what that builds? Trust, my friends – the secret sauce to creating a squad of die-hard fans.

Now, you're probably wondering, "How do I turn my brand from an experience to having a fan club that rivals a rock band's?" Well, it's like building a house – you got to start with a darn good foundation. So, grab your hard hat and let's dig deep, right down to the roots of it all. Ready for a journey that'll make your brand a headliner in the fan club world? Let's dive in

2

Understanding Your Brand

Before you unleash your brand magic, you've got to dive into the mystical depths of what makes it tick. Think of it as the ultimate quest where you'll unravel the secrets of your brand, from its core values to the epic mission and vision it carries. Picture it like crafting your brand's own superhero origin story. Now, buckle up, because we're about to embark on a brand audit adventure and decipher the enigma that is your target audience. It's like being a brand detective – who lives on 221b Baker Street, with a touch of glamour.

To dig deep into the heart of your brand, here are five questions that will guide you through the labyrinth:

1. What values do you want your brand to embody?
2. What's the mission that fuels your brand's journey?
3. Can you clearly visualize the vision your brand aspires to achieve?
4. Who is your target audience, and what makes them tick?
5. How can a brand audit uncover hidden gems and areas for improvement

3

Creating a Unique Brand Identity

Alright, picture this: when I kick off a branding gig, I don't just jump into colors and logos – oh no, I start with a deep dive. I hit my clients with this questionnaire that's like the detective work of the branding world. Why? Because before you jazz up your visuals, you have to know the soul of your business – the values and goals that make it tick.

Now, this questionnaire of mine is no light read; it's a heavy-weight champion packed with questions that dig into the nitty-gritty. We're talking values, goals, target market vibes, style preferences – the whole shebang.

Why does this matter so much, you ask? Well, think of your values as the North Star of your business galaxy. They guide everything – how you show up, how you shout about your awesomeness, and how you connect with the world. Get clear on these, and you've got yourself a compass for the wild business journey.

Let me share one of my book shopping experiences with you. I'm strolling into a cozy bookstore, and I'm not just your average reader – I'm on a mission to pick the perfect book. What is my book-picking philosophy you ask? Honesty is my jam. Right from the first chapter, I'm all about those face-to-face recommendations with the friendly bookstore clerk. No hiding behind book blurbs or generic reviews. I want the real talk, the inside scoop. And I carry that honesty torch through the whole bookish journey, encouraging the clerk to spill their thoughts and bookish ideas.

And guess what happens? It's like a literary magic spell – these bookish interactions become a delightful dance. I discover books I otherwise may have never read, I found a clerk who provided a meaningful engagement of value, and I left the bookstore having an enjoyable experience. That my friends is called the ultimate bookish win – mission accomplished!

So, why spill the beans on this little bookstore adventure and how does it tie into building a brand identity? Well, let me unravel this literary tale for you. This wasn't your run-of-the-mill bookstore – it wasn't just a snazzy logo or a shop with a catchy name. No, no. It was a haven where the bookish magic came alive, and it all started with the book whisperer behind the counter.

The moment I popped the question, "Hey, what's a must-read?" boom! The bookstore clerk's eyes light up like a well-written plot twist. You could practically feel the excitement radiating from this book guru. Now, that's the kind of spirit I want on my bookish dream team, representing the heart and soul of my literary haven.

The bookstores niche – was all about indie and self-published gems. And this clerk? A walking encyclopedia of these hidden wordsmiths. The way he effortlessly connected with people over these books was pure magic. He wasn't just recommending books; he was weaving a tapestry of connections, introducing readers to stories that spoke to their souls.

In my book (pun intended), he embodies the very identity of that bookstore. The passion for literature, the deep dive into indie treasures, the ability to connect hearts through books – that's the brand identity right there, no questions asked. So, if you're out to create a brand that's not just a name but a living, breathing entity, find your equivalent of the bookstore whisperer. Someone who doesn't just sell, but weaves stories and connections, making your brand come alive. Now go out there and let your brand story be as unforgettable as a plot twist in a well-crafted novel!

Takeaway time: Questions you must be able to answer to ensure your business is tougher than superhero armor.

1. Who's your dream squad – the people you want to serve?
2. What's your secret sauce – the thing you rock at?
3. How are you different from your competitors?
4. And, of course, what values are your guiding stars?

Answer these, and you're on your way to a brand that's not just seen but remembered. Now go conquer those branding dreams! And remember people want to connect to people!

4

Building a Consistent Brand Image

Alright, let's chat about the glue that holds the branding universe together – consistency. My favorite bookstore wouldn't be as enchanting if it had a different vibe every time you stepped in, right? The same goes for your brand. We're diving into the secrets of keeping that vibe rock-solid across every channel, from the online realm to the good ol' offline spaces.

So, how do you pull off this branding magic trick? It's a three-step dance: brand guidelines, style guides, and a bit of employee training pizzazz.

Brand Guidelines: Think of this as your brand's rulebook, the sacred scripture that lays down the law on how your brand struts its stuff. It's not just about the logo – it's the color palette, the tone of voice, and the personality quirks that make your brand uniquely yours.

If you're having trouble picking colors, let's simmer down the color palette chaos and think simplicity. Imagine your brand as a canvas, and you're picking just 2 or 3 colors to be the rockstars. The rest? Well, they're the background dancers, there to add a little flair and make those main colors shine. It's like curating your own visual symphony – pick the lead instruments, and let the others harmonize. So, instead of drowning in a sea of colors, let's pick a couple to steal the spotlight and let the others play the supporting role.

If you're caught in a color tug-of-war and feeling a bit undecided, here's a simple trick: opt for something neutral and start your journey from there. Neutrals are like the calm waters in a sea of options, giving you a steady base to dive into the colorful possibilities. So, if the rainbow is overwhelming, let neutrality be your compass to guide you through the spectrum.

Style Guides: Now, this is like the fashion magazine of your brand. It breaks down the nitty-gritty – fonts, imagery, layouts – all the visual bling that keeps your brand looking sharp and recognizable. Whether you're strutting down the website runway or lighting up social platforms, cohesion is the name of the game. Keep that look, feel, and vibe as tight knit as a book club discussing a plot twist.

Now, pay attention to the nuances here – it's not just about the visuals; we're talking about the "feel" and "vibe." This is where your brand personality comes alive. It's in how you spill the tea about yourself, the way you chat up your audience, the language you sling, and the dance you do with your interactions.

So, whether you're posting on the socials, tweeting up a storm, or ruling your website domain, let it all harmonize. Your brand should be like a well-rehearsed orchestra – every note, every interaction, creating a symphony that's uniquely yours. Ready to rock that cohesive brand presence? Let's make your online stage a place where your brand shines bright and unmistakable!

Employee Training: Now, thinking back to my cozy bookstore. If the beloved friendly clerk suddenly transformed into a sci-fi guru overnight, it'd be like turning a page to a completely different story. Definitely not the plot twist I signed up for, huh? That's where the secret sauce comes in – training. We're not talking about rocket science; it's about ensuring every member of your brand squad is grooving to the same beat. It's like creating a melody where each employee dances to the brand rhythm by heart. Remember people want to connect with people, so make sure your training reflects your brands missions and vision clearly.

In a nutshell, it's about making sure that whether your brand is waltzing through the online world or doing a cha-cha at a live event, it's doing it with the same swagger. So, if you want your brand to be as consistent as your go-to comfort read, follow this three-step groove, and you'll have your brand dancing in harmony across the whole stage!

Takeaway time: Your style basics check list should include the following.

- Style
- Forms
- Fonts
- Copyrighting

- Aesthetics
- Shapes
- Colors
- Tagline
- Imagery

5

Crafting Compelling Brand Stories

Alright, let's unravel the magic of storytelling in the world of branding. We're diving deep into how tales can be the heartstrings that connect your brand with your audience. We're not just talking about any stories; we're delving into the art of crafting brand narratives that don't just speak, but sing to your audience, creating emotional bonds that last.

Now, let me spin you a yarn – imagine you're kick starting your health coaching venture. Your audience isn't just after tips; they crave a story, a journey. Share the ups, the downs, spill the secrets you've gathered on your wellness path. Because, here's the thing, people want to engage with a story, and guess what? You're the author of your brand's story. People want to connect to people.

Be the health guru who's been there, done that, and is rocking the T-shirt. It's about being yourself, embracing your quirks, and owning your expertise. Even if your business is fresh on the block, dish out what you know with honesty, generosity, and that ever-helpful attitude. Remember that honesty torch I mentioned earlier? Well, it's your guiding light. Just like I trust the bookstore for recommendations, your customers will want to trust you for your insights.

So, here's the plot twist: whether you're in wellness, tech, or dog grooming – share your wisdom – share you! Your audience wants the real deal. Be the genuine article, stand out from the crowd, and let your expertise shine. Your customers aren't just buying a product; they're investing in a story they believe in, and that, my friend, is the power of your brand tale.

Takeaway time: Brand photos should include the following.

- Headshot
- Team Photos
- Casual Portraits
- Product or Service Photos
- Lifestyle Portraits
- Location or on Scene Photos
- Creative Stills
- Event Coverage
- Photos of Celebrations (Anniversary/Milestone)
- Customer Testimonials

6

Leveraging Digital Platforms

Having a digital presence isn't just important; it's like the oxygen for your brand. So, what's the game plan? First and foremost, our website is the grand entrance to your digital business mansion. Its where curious minds stroll in to discover who you are, the essence of your business, the juicy details of your services, and how to kickstart a collaboration. In today's world, it's practically your digital business card – and you know what they say about first impressions.

Especially when you're just kicking off, that website of yours is your command center. It's where you direct the traffic, flaunt your goods, and, most importantly, gather intel from potential clients. Now, if growing your newsletter squad is on the agenda, here's the secret sauce – whip up a tempting opt-in. Something that's so irresistible, people can't help but snatch it up and dive into your world. It's like the golden ticket to join your exclusive club – and who wouldn't want to be a part of that? So, let's make sure your website isn't just a place on the internet; it's a magnetic force pulling people into your business wonderland.

Now, let's talk about the magic of thoughtful and strategic curation for social media– it's like the secret sauce that can elevate your brand messaging and storytelling. In a world bombarded with messages, options, and choices every single day, the brands that stand out are the ones that embrace mindful curation. Picture this: it's like sipping a perfectly crafted coffee after drowning in a sea of choices at a mega café.

Curation is your shield against the overwhelming chaos of too many options. You know that feeling when you're faced with an endless menu, and you end up panicking and settling for a side salad and breadsticks? Yeah, no fun. Now, think about those brands that keep it simple, with a curated menu of offerings, a consistent vibe, and a well-defined aesthetic. Those are the brands we fall head over heels for – whether it's the artisan doughnut shop, the small batch distillery, or the homewares haven with its carefully selected handmade pottery collection.

What ties these beloved brands together? It's that secret weapon called consistent and thoughtful curation, coupled with a compelling story. It's a game-changer, my friends. Pouring energy into curation isn't just a whim; it's a strategic move. The more we invest in curating our brand, the more others perceive it exactly the way we intended – a masterpiece crafted with precision and purpose.

7

Engaging with Your Audience

Let's dive into the art of community building and explore strategies to connect with your audience through social media, customer feedback, and various interactive methods. Imagine yourself as the dynamic host, the soul of the brand party. Social media transcends being a mere platform; it's your virtual dance floor where your brand flaunts its moves and sparks conversations that could rival a parrot's chat. Treat your audience like VIPs – respond to comments, throw in questions, and keep the banter flowing. But our journey doesn't end there; customer feedback becomes your exclusive pass to the backstage revelations. Customer feedback functions as your undercover agents, uncovering audience thoughts in a treasure trove of insights. Infuse some interactive flair – quizzes, polls, live sessions – it's akin to tossing sparklers into your brand's party mix. It's more than engagement; it's curating an experience where your audience isn't just spectators but active contributors to the brand bash. So, cue the confetti, my fellow brand revelers, because we're transforming audience engagement into the starring act of our brand extravaganza!

Takeaway time: Here is a sample framework for creating a captivating audience engagement experience.

Authentic Conversations:

1. Objective: Build a genuine connection with your audience.
2. Activities:

- Respond promptly to comments and messages on social media.
- Share behind-the-scenes glimpses to humanize your brand.
- Encourage user-generated content by showcasing customer experiences.

Strategic Questioning:

1. Objective: Spark meaningful conversations and gather valuable insights.
2. Activities:

- Pose thought-provoking questions to encourage audience participation.
- Run Q&A sessions or polls to gauge opinions and preferences.
- Utilize open-ended questions to foster dialogue and showcase brand personality.

Banter and Wit:

1. Objective: Infuse humor and personality into your interactions.

2. Activities:

- Craft witty responses that align with your brand tone.
- Share lighthearted content and memes that resonate with your audience.
- Embrace meme culture and internet trends for relatable content.

Customer Feedback Utilization:

1. Objective: Leverage feedback to enhance the brand experience.
2. Activities:

- Acknowledge and appreciate positive feedback publicly.
- Address negative feedback with transparency and a commitment to improvement.
- Implement changes based on recurring themes in customer suggestions.

Interactive Content:

1. Objective: Transform your brand into an interactive playground.
2. Activities:

- Create engaging quizzes that align with your brand's personality.
- Host live sessions for product demos, Q&A, or behind-the-scenes tours.
- Run polls to involve your audience in decision-making

processes.

Surprise and Delight Campaigns:

1. Objective: Create memorable and unexpected moments for your audience.
2. Activities:

- Organize surprise giveaways or contests.
- Send personalized messages or exclusive offers to loyal customers.
- Celebrate special occasions or milestones with your audience.

Exclusive Communities:

1. Objective: Foster a sense of belonging among your audience.
2. Activities:

- Create private groups or forums for dedicated fans.
- Offer exclusive content or early access to new products/services for community members.
- Facilitate connections among audience members to strengthen the community.

Multi-Platform Engagement:

1. Objective: Reach your audience wherever they are.
2. Activities:

- Tailor content for various platforms, considering the unique characteristics of each.
- Cross-promote content across different channels to maximize reach.
- Collaborate with influencers or partners to tap into new audiences.

Consistent Brand Persona:

1. Objective: Reinforce your brand identity through consistent engagement.
2. Activities:

- Maintain a unified brand voice across all interactions.
- Ensure visuals, messaging, and interactions align with your brand personality.
- Incorporate brand elements into interactive content for instant recognition.

Adapt and Evolve:

1. **Objective:** Stay agile and responsive to changing audience dynamics.
2. **Activities:**

- Monitor audience trends and preferences.
- Integrate emerging platforms and communication styles.
- Regularly assess the success of engagement strategies and iterate as needed.

8

Challenges and Solutions

Let's be real – building a brand comes with its fair share of challenges. We're here to unpack the common roadblocks businesses often encounter on their journey to brand greatness. But fear not, because we're not just pointing out the hurdles; we're handing you a toolbox of practical solutions to leap over them. Because in the world of branding, every challenge is just a chance to showcase your superhero skills.

1: Unleashing Unshakable Confidence: There are a bunch of reasons why even the savviest business minds sometimes struggle to unleash their full confidence. But here's the game-changer – from confidently selecting brand colors to rocking presentations, it all comes down to a mindset makeover. Whether you're diving into body language courses, entrepreneurial training, or exploring other confidence-boosting methods, the key lies in unearthing that unshakeable confidence within you. It's not just about what you know; it's about how you carry that knowledge with the unwavering belief that you're owning the game.

2: Securing Resources: Diving right into the real talk for our fellow small business champs and entrepreneurs – the funding hustle is no joke. But fear not, because where there's a will, there's a way! Getting creative is the name of the game. Ever thought about rallying your tribe with crowdfunding, cozying up to private investors, or even donning the cape of self-funding? These are your unconventional allies in the quest for financial backing.

Now, here's a golden nugget of advice – grants. Consider them the unicorns of the funding world, offering free money that can be a game-changer. Don't let a rejection on your first grant application rain on your parade; there are thousands out there waiting to be explored. It's like a treasure hunt – apply, apply often, and you might just strike gold.

3: Niche Mastery: Let's talk about conquering the market realm. Here's the deal – you want to cast your net wide, but reality check, not everyone's going to be head over heels for what you offer. That's where the magic of finding and serving the ideal client comes in. Now, I get it – the idea of narrowing down your market might sound like scaling down the mountain but hear me out.

Targeting a small niche isn't about limiting yourself; it's about unleashing a powerhouse of opportunities for your business. It's like having a secret garden of potential clients who are not just interested but invested in what you bring to the table. And guess what? This is a hurdle every company grapples with finding its sweet spot in the market. The key here is to own your space and let everything else fall into its groove – not just in terms of branding, but in the entire symphony of your business.

4: Work-Life Balance: Ah, the delicate dance of work-life balance – a challenge many of us face in the hustle and bustle of the entrepreneurial world. It's like juggling flaming torches, but fear not, my fellow business warriors, for achieving balance is not an elusive unicorn. It starts with setting clear boundaries, knowing when to power down the laptop and savor the non-work moments. Embrace the magic of prioritization; not everything needs a spot on your to-do list. Learn the art of saying no when your plate is full, and don't forget to sprinkle self-care into your daily routine. It's not about perfect balance but finding a rhythm that keeps you in sync with both your professional and personal worlds. So, let's swap the juggling act for a carefully choreographed dance, were work and life waltz together harmoniously.

9

Measuring Success

Diving into the realm of customer loyalty is akin to deciphering the intricate notes of a symphony. It's more than just tracking repeat purchases; it's about understanding the melody that keeps customers returning for an encore. Start by scrutinizing the frequency of purchases, but don't stop there – delve into the qualitative realm, exploring customer reviews and feedback. Measure the consistency of engagement across various touch points, from social media interactions to customer service encounters. Customer loyalty isn't a static snapshot; it's a dynamic interplay of experiences. Conduct surveys to gauge customer satisfaction and analyze patterns to discern what keeps them devoted to your brand. Remember, the true essence of loyalty lies not just in the transactional dance but in the emotional connection that transforms a customer into a brand enthusiast. So, let's orchestrate a strategy that not only retains customers but transforms them into lifelong aficionados of your brand symphony.

Embarking on the analysis of market share is akin to navigating the vast landscape of a bustling marketplace. It's not merely about claiming a slice; it's about understanding the intricate dance of your brand amid competitors. Begin by crunching the numbers, gauging the percentage of total sales within your industry. But market share analysis extends beyond quantitative metrics; it delves into the qualitative tapestry of consumer perceptions. Dive into customer feedback, scrutinize reviews, and grasp the sentiment surrounding your brand in comparison to others. Explore the dynamics of market growth and contraction, keeping a keen eye on emerging trends. It's not just about having a share; it's about actively shaping and expanding that share by aligning with consumer needs and staying ahead in the ever-evolving market symphony. So, let's navigate this marketplace waltz, ensuring our brand not only claims its space but dances to a tune that resonates with the audience.

Navigating the success metrics of brand equality involves a journey beyond the conventional yardsticks. It's not solely about crunching numbers, but about discerning impact and resonance. Begin by gauging the diversity and inclusivity within your team, ensuring a mosaic of voices shapes your brand narrative. Extend your measurement to the wider community, actively seeking feedback on how your brand connects with diverse audiences. Scrutinize customer engagement and feedback across demographics, deciphering whether your brand message transcends borders. The triumph of brand equality transcends mere financial gains; it's embedded in the authenticity of connections forged and the brand's role as a stalwart advocate for diversity and inclusion. The true measure lies in fostering a culture where everyone feels acknowledged, valued, and empowered – an intangible success that defines brand equality.

27

10

Monitoring and Adapting

Navigating the realm of branding is a perpetual voyage that demands unwavering vigilance and adaptability. This section as a treasure trove of tools and metrics – an entire superhero utility belt crafted for the sole purpose of tracking your brand's performance. Meet the classics, like Google Analytics, your trusty digital sidekick unraveling the mysteries of website traffic and user behavior. Don't forget about social media management tools. They're your steadfast wingmen, helping trace engagement and audience vibes. And hold on, because we're not just scratching the surface; customer feedback platforms are the undercover agents, divulging what the people genuinely think. The pièce de résistance? Brand sentiment analysis tools, decoding the mood around your brand like a digital-age mood ring. It's not just tracking; it's a data-driven fiesta where every metric is a dance move, aiming to keep the audience cheering for an encore. So, strap in, my fellow brand enthusiasts, because we're gearing up to transform data into the rockstar anthem of our brand's triumph!

Takeaway time: The following is a sample framework outlining nine essential business facets for monitoring.

Continuous Assessment:

1. Objective: Keep a finger on the pulse of your brand's performance.
2. Activities:

- Regularly review social media analytics to gauge engagement and sentiment.
- Utilize web analytics tools to track website traffic, bounce rates, and user behavior.
- Implement customer feedback mechanisms to capture real-time insights.

Social Media Engagement:

1. Objective: Leverage social platforms as a dynamic space for brand interaction.
2. Activities:

- Monitor comments, direct messages, and mentions for immediate response.
- Analyze social media trends to align your brand's messaging and content.

Feedback Analysis:

1. Objective: Turn customer feedback into actionable improvements.

2. Activities:

- Regularly analyze customer reviews on various platforms.
- Conduct surveys and gather feedback through customer support channels.
- Categorize feedback into positive and negative insights for strategic adjustments.

Key Performance Indicators (KPIs):

1. Objective: Track specific metrics aligning with business objectives.
2. Activities:

- Identify KPIs relevant to brand goals (e.g., conversion rates, brand mentions).
- Set benchmarks and regularly assess performance against these benchmarks.

Competitor Analysis:

1. Objective: Stay aware of industry trends and competitive positioning.
2. Activities:

- Regularly analyze competitors' branding strategies and messaging.
- Identify gaps or opportunities based on competitor strengths and weaknesses.

Flexibility in Messaging:

1. Objective: Adapt brand messaging based on real-time trends and audience response.
2. Activities:

- Stay informed about current events and cultural shifts.
- Be flexible in adapting messaging to maintain relevance and resonance.

Regular Strategy Reviews:

1. Objective: Ensure brand strategy aligns with broader business goals.
2. Activities:

- Conduct periodic reviews of brand strategy against market changes.
- Adjust the brand strategy based on the evolving business landscape.

Community Engagement:

1. Objective: Foster a sense of community around the brand.
2. Activities:

- Organize and participate in events that resonate with your audience.
- Facilitate user-generated content and celebrate customer stories.

Crisis Preparedness:

1. Objective: Be ready to navigate and mitigate potential crises.
2. Activities:

- Develop a crisis communication plan.
- Regularly review and update the plan based on industry insights and trends.

11

Conclusion

In the grand finale, brand crafting – it's not a one-hit wonder, more like a blockbuster sequel with ongoing twists and turns. It's a recipe: sprinkle in meticulous planning, a dash of boundless creativity, and just enough flexibility to pirouette through surprises. Use this guide as your backstage pass to crafting a brand that's not just strong, but practically sing to your audience. It's like building the brand version of a rockstar – enduring, charming, and always ready for an encore. So, saddle up, follow these epic strategies, and create a brand story that doesn't just resonate, but leaves 'em roaring for an encore!

12

Resources

Coffin, S. (2023, May 23). *10 Must-Have Photos for your Small business Photo Shoot.* Sara Coffin Photo. https://saracoffinphoto .com/10-must-have-photos-for-your-small-business-photo-shoot/

Rafiq, R. (2022, September 5). *Branding for Beginners: How to get started — R Artspace.* R Artspace. https://www.rartspace.com/bl og/branding-for-beginners-how-to-get-started?utm_conten t=smartloop&utm_term=6731518&pp=1